Zoom, Zoom, Zoom

Written by Kirsten Hall

Illustrated by Viviana Garofoli

children's press ®

A Division of Scholastic Inc.
New York Toronto London Auckland Sydney
Mexico City New Delhi Hong Kong
Danbury, Connecticut

Library of Congress Cataloging-in-Publication Data

Hall, Kirsten.
  Zoom, zoom, zoom / written by Kirsten Hall ; illustrated by Viviana Garofoli.
      p. cm.
Summary: A young boy imagines himself driving all around the town while playing with his new toy car.
  ISBN 0-516-24414-0 (lib. bdg.)   0-516-25509-6 (pbk.)
  [1. Automobile driving–Fiction.] I. Garófoli, Viviana, ill. II.
Title.
  PZ7.H1457Zo 2004
  [E]–dc22
                              2003013985

1 2 3 4 5 6 7 8 9 10 R 13 12 11 10 09 08 07 06 05 04

Note to Parents and Teachers

Once a reader can recognize and identify the 23 words used to tell this story, he or she will be able to successfully read the entire book. These 23 words are repeated throughout the story, so that young readers will be able to recognize the words easily and understand their meaning.

The 23 words used in this book are:

at	in	right
back	it	room
car	just	slow
drive	left	the
far	my	to
fast	near	watch
go	new	zoom
I	night	

4

Zoom, zoom, zoom.

5

I drive in my new car.

I drive my new car near.

I drive my new car far.

12

Zoom, zoom, zoom.

I drive my new car slow.

I drive my new car fast.

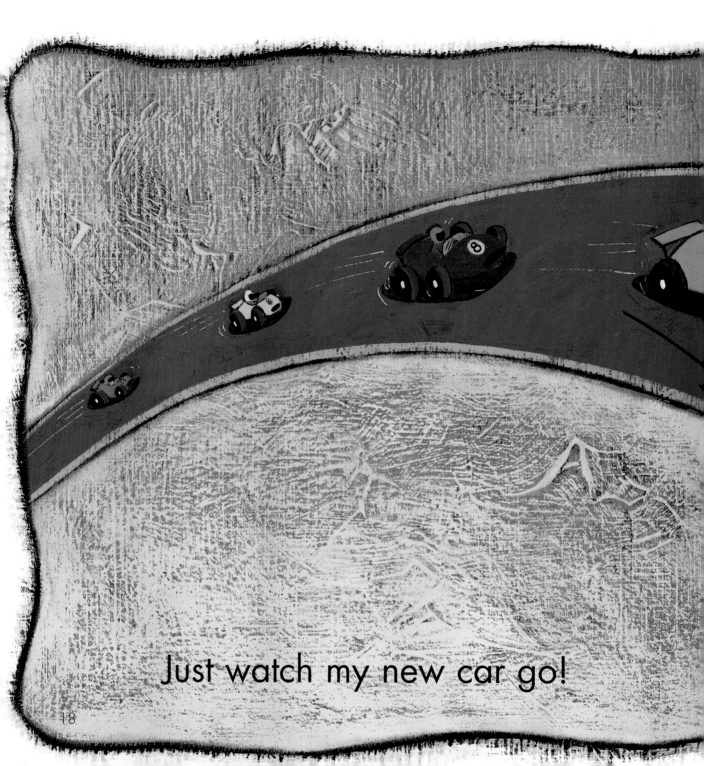

Just watch my new car go!

Zoom, zoom, zoom.

I drive my car at night.

I drive it to the left.

I drive it to the right.

Zoom, zoom, zoom.

I drive back to my room.

ABOUT THE AUTHOR

Kirsten Hall has lived most of her life in New York City. While she was still in high school, she published her first book for children, *Bunny, Bunny*. Since then, she has written and published more than sixty children's books. Hall wrote *Zoom, Zoom, Zoom* because she loves to drive cars herself—especially backward! A former early education teacher, Kirsten currently works as a children's book editor.

ABOUT THE ILLUSTRATOR

As a child, **Viviana Garofoli's** favorite pastime was playing with watercolors and crayons on big sheets of paper. If asked what she wanted to be when she grew up, she would reply, "A painter." Garofoli graduated from Escuela Nacional de Bellas Artes Pridiliano Pueyrredon with a degree in fine arts. After exhibiting her work at numerous galleries, she started illustrating for the publishing market. For the last fifteen years, Garofoli has dedicated all her time to illustrating children's books and now has more than twenty to her credit. She currently lives in Buenos Aires, Argentina, with her husband, Sergio, and daughter, April.